LEADERSHIP BEYOND RANK AND POWER

THEOLOGY OF WORK PROJECT

LEADERSHIP
BEYOND
RANK AND POWER

THE BIBLE AND YOUR WORK
Study Series

HENDRICKSON PUBLISHERS

Theology of Work
The Bible and Your Work Study Series
Leadership beyond Rank and Power

© 2017 by Hendrickson Publishers Marketing, LLC
P.O. Box 3473
Peabody, Massachusetts 01961-3473
www.hendrickson.com

ISBN 978-1-61970-979-9

Adapted from the *Theology of Work Bible Commentary*, copyright © 2014 by the Theology of Work Project, Inc. All rights reserved.

All Scripture quotations, unless otherwise indicated, are taken from the Holy Bible, English Standard Version (ESV®), copyright © 2001, by Crossway, a publishing ministry of Good News Publishers. Used by permission. All rights reserved.

Scripture quotations marked (NIV) are taken from the Holy Bible, New International Version®, NIV®. Copyright © 1973, 1978, 1984, 2011 by Biblica, Inc.™ Used by permission of Zondervan. All rights reserved worldwide. www.zondervan.com. The "NIV" and "New International Version" are trademarks registered in the United States Patent and Trademark Office by Biblica, Inc.™

Scripture quotations marked (NASB) are taken from the New American Standard Bible®, Copyright © 1960, 1962, 1963, 1968, 1971, 1972, 1973, 1975, 1977, 1995 by The Lockman Foundation. Used by permission. (www.lockman.org)

William Messenger, Executive Editor, Theology of Work Project
Sean McDonough, Biblical Editor, Theology of Work Project
Patricia Anders, Editorial Director, Hendrickson Publishers

Contributors:

Valerie O'Connell, "Leadership beyond Rank and Power" Bible Study
Darrell L. Bock, "Beyond Rank and Power: What Philemon Tells Us about Leadership," Theology of Work Project article

The Theology of Work Project is an independent, international organization dedicated to researching, writing, and distributing materials with a biblical perspective on work. The Project's primary mission is to produce resources covering every book of the Bible plus major topics in today's workplaces. Wherever possible, the Project collaborates with other faith-and-work organizations, churches, universities and seminaries to help equip people for meaningful, productive work of every kind.

Printed in the United States of America

First Printing—July 2017

Contents

The Theology of Work — vii

Introduction — 1

1. Paul's Leadership Skills at Work
Lesson #1: The Leadership Challenge — 3
Lesson #2: Paul's Approach — 6
Lesson #3: It's Personal in Every Direction — 9

2. Jesus Is a Leveler of Rank, Power, and Social Status
Lesson #1: From Slave to Brother to Apostle — 12
Lesson #2: Brotherhood Is a Two-Way Street — 15
Lesson #3: Specialized Functions in One Body with Many Members — 17

3. Leadership Is Grounded in Relationships
Lesson #1: Relationships at Work — 20
Lesson #2: Image-Bearers at Work — 23
Lesson #3: Technology and Relationships — 26

4. Leadership in Action
Lesson #1: Leaders Grow People — 29
Lesson #2: Leaders Exert Authority — 31
Lesson #3: Leaders Bear the Cost — 34

5. Leadership Is Service
Lesson #1: Leaders Are Servants — 37
Lesson #2: Leaders in Service — 39
Lesson #3: Servant Leaders Trust God's Provision — 42

6. Leadership in Difficult Times
Lesson #1: Leaders Face Opposition — 45
Lesson #2: Leaders Stay the Course — 48
Lesson #3: Leaders Fail — 50

7. The Impact of Leadership
Lesson #1: Leaders Bring Good and Evil — 53
Lesson #2: Leaders Build Leaders — 55
Lesson #3: Leaders Resolve Conflicts — 58

8. Truth, Love, Trust, and Effectiveness
Lesson #1: Truth and Love Build Trust — 61
Lesson #2: Trust and Transparency Build Effectiveness — 64
Lesson #3: Godly Leadership Is Effective Leadership — 67

Wisdom for Using This Study in the Workplace — 71

Leader's Guide — 73

The Theology of Work

Work is not only a human calling, but also a divine one. "In the beginning God created the heavens and the earth." God worked to create us and created us to work. "The Lord God took the man and put him in the garden of Eden to work it and keep it" (Gen. 2:15). God also created work to be good, even if it's hard to see in a fallen world. To this day, God calls us to work to support ourselves and to serve others (Eph. 4:28).

Work can accomplish many of God's purposes for our lives—the basic necessities of food and shelter, as well as a sense of fulfillment and joy. Our work can create ways to help people thrive; it can discover the depths of God's creation; and it can bring us into wonderful relationships with co-workers and those who benefit from our work (customers, clients, patients, and so forth).

Yet many people face drudgery, boredom, or exploitation at work. We have bad bosses, hostile relationships, and unfriendly work environments. Our work seems useless, unappreciated, faulty, and frustrating. We don't get paid enough. We get stuck in dead-end jobs or laid off or fired. We fail. Our skills become obsolete. It's a struggle just to make ends meet. But how can this be if God created work to be good—and what can we do about it? God's answers for these questions must be somewhere in the Bible, but where?

The Theology of Work Project's mission has been to study what the Bible says about work and to develop resources to apply the Christian faith to our work. It turns out that every book of the Bible gives practical, relevant guidance that can help us do our jobs better, improve our relationships at work, support ourselves, serve others more effectively, and find meaning and value in our work. The Bible shows us how to live all of life—including *work*—in Christ. Only in Jesus can we and our work be transformed to become the blessing it was always meant to be.

To put it another way, if we are not following Christ during the 100,000 hours of our lives that we spend at work, are we really following Christ? Our lives are more than just one day a week at church. The fact is that God cares about our life *every day of the week*. But how do we become equipped to follow Jesus at work? In the same ways we become equipped for every aspect of life in Christ—listening to sermons, modeling our lives on others' examples, praying for God's guidance, and most of all by studying the Bible and putting it into practice.

This Theology of Work series contains a variety of books to help you apply the Scriptures and Christian faith to your work. This Bible study is one volume in the series The Bible and Your Work. It is intended for those who want to explore what the Bible says about work and how to apply it to their work in positive, practical ways. Although it can be used for individual study, Bible study is especially effective with a group of people committed to practicing what they read in Scripture. In this way, we gain from one another's perspectives and are encouraged to actually *do* what we read in Scripture. Because of the direct focus on work, The Bible and Your Work studies are especially suited for Bible studies *at* work or *with* other people in similar occupations. The following lessons are designed for thirty-minute lunch breaks (or perhaps breakfast before work) during a five-day work week.

Christians today recognize God's calling for us in and through our work—for ourselves and for those whom we serve. May God use this book to help you follow Christ in every sphere of life and work.

Will Messenger, Executive Editor
Theology of Work Project

Introduction

Today's leader lives in a fast-paced world of complexity, diversity, and conflicting objectives. Whether a CEO, second shift supervisor, project manager, team leader, or simply a person that others choose to follow, a leader has specific goals to achieve or surpass. A leader applies his or her best efforts for the sake of his or her shareholders, constituents, employees, congregation, or employer. The leader who is a Christian believer is also driven by a commitment to serving the Lord Jesus first. Many leaders struggle with reconciling the demands of the marketplace with the eternal values of their faith. What if these mandates conflict?

This Bible study will conclude that there is no native conflict for the leader who actively engages the full arsenal of Christ-like values, attitudes, and behaviors. To reach this conclusion, the study is grounded in Paul's letter to Philemon. Through Philemon, we identify some key points about leadership and explore them in action—both in the Old Testament and in modern times. The purpose of this study is to refresh participants' understanding of how God views their work, and to encourage them in their exercise of leadership that is both godly and effective.

Weighing in at just 355 Greek words, Philemon is the shortest book written by Paul and one of the shortest in the entire New Testament. It is so short that it doesn't even have chapters, so verse references are given as, for example, Philemon 1. Given its brevity, the inclusion of this letter in the canon of Scripture might initially seem surprising. But this short Epistle packs a powerful message as it models some very effective leadership qualities. These qualities are foundational to Christians who need to actively live out their faith in a productive and profitable workplace.

This brief Epistle is addressed to Philemon, a believing slave owner, who is well-known to Paul. The occasion of the letter is the hastening return of Philemon's slave Onesimus who has either run away or sought out Paul for some undisclosed purpose. Slavery was an economic and social reality of the time in which Paul writes and he makes no judgment about the institution. Rather, slavery forms the context for Paul's approach to social roles and for the profound change knowing Jesus should bring. Paul deals with themes related to power, rank, justice, and mercy. How Paul handles the conflict between Philemon and Onesimus reveals that faith in Jesus changes all aspects of life, including the role of leadership and the use of power.

Chapter 1
Paul's Leadership Skills at Work

Lesson #1: The Leadership Challenge

Although we don't know the back story of how and why Onesimus came to be with Paul in his captivity, we do know that the slave owner Philemon was most likely not part of that plan. Whatever the initial cause, a compelling result was that the slave had himself become a believer in Jesus, a beloved and valuable helper—a brother in Christ to Paul, and by extension, a brother in Christ to Philemon his wronged master.

By running away or seeking Paul's help in a dispute with Philemon, Onesimus had deprived his master of his services. This wrong resulted in a social and economic debt. As the owner of a slave who had run away, Philemon holds all of the social and legal power. Paul addresses Philemon as one who has several choices about how to proceed.

Paul's greeting to Philemon sets the stage for a delicate social negotiation. He opens by commending Philemon's love and faith, prayerfully reminding the man of their shared priority—"the good that we may do for Christ" (Philem. 6). This greeting establishes a practical relationship as a basis for decision making and action. The Greek word fellowship (*koinōnia*) is a word that describes a participation, a joint interacting and engagement with others. It is active, not passive. This is the sort of active participation that Paul hopes to stir in Philemon with the letter's opening sentences.

Paul has realistic reason to be hopeful of a positive resolution to the conflict, because Philemon's track record shows he had been a cause of refreshment to the hearts of saints. There are seven verses before Paul begins to make a single request. They are not simply opening remarks, casual comments, or even flattery. They are constructed to lay the foundation for Paul's request and act as arguments for the request to be granted.

We don't know the exact nature of Paul's request beyond that Philemon welcomes Onesimus back as he would welcome Paul himself. And we don't know how Philemon responded to Paul's letter, although we later find Paul sending Onesimus "our faithful and beloved brother" with Tychicus to the Colossians (Col. 4:7–9). So, at the very least, Philemon clearly did not exercise his power to do away with the wayward slave. Onesimus continued in his faith and in his association with Paul and usefulness to the kingdom.

Food for Thought

Slavery was an established institution in both Roman society and Jewish tradition. Unlike later slavery in the United States, the ancient version was unrelated to race. During the American Civil War, both slave owners and abolitionists used this Epistle to bolster their point of view. Paul doesn't take issue with the institution or with Philemon's rights but asserts the need for active fellowship. How is active fellowship possible in the context of slavery? How does this relate to rank or position in the workplace?

_____

_____

_____

_____

_____

_____

_____

_____

Think of a time when you have been wronged and someone asked you to give up your power in that regard. What arguments were used? What did you decide? And how did you feel afterward? What part did your beliefs play in the transaction?

_____

_____

_____

_____

_____

_____

_____

_____

Prayer

Father God,

I come to you with an open heart to learn how to become a leader who honors you in all ways. Please help me to not only learn, but to obey your teachings with a willing spirit.

Amen.

Lesson #2: Paul's Approach

In this Epistle, Paul builds an architecture of relationships and obligations that is founded on Jesus Christ. "Paul, a prisoner of Jesus Christ . . ." is the opening salvo (Philem. 1). He is literally a prisoner of Christ, in prison because of Christ and under the complete control of Christ in service of him and his kingdom.

As such, his "dear friend" Philemon is a "co-worker" (Philem. 1), albeit a free one in the comforts of the church that meets in his house. This contrast sets up an obligation as both a friend and co-worker in the purposes of "God our Father and the Lord Jesus Christ" (Philem. 3). Paul commends Philemon for past services and for loving Jesus. In so doing Paul reminds Philemon that the purpose of all efforts is to be increasingly effective in doing good for Christ. When effectiveness of service is the top priority, an individual's rank takes a backseat.

Having set their shared priorities firmly in place, Paul turns to the matter of authority. Hierarchically, Paul asserts his power to "command" Philemon to do his "duty" (Philem. 8). But he puts that power aside, preferring to "appeal to you on the basis of love" (Philem. 9). In putting aside his right of command due his rank, Paul models the behavior that he wants to elicit from Philemon. He hopes that Philemon will equally lay down his rights as slave owner.

Paul continues saying, "and I, Paul, do this as an old man, and now as a prisoner of Jesus Christ" (Philem. 9). With this declaration, Paul is claiming the respect rightly due a Jewish elder, as well as reinforcing the plight of his imprisonment for their mutual Lord. Paul will make the request on the basis of love "in order that your good deed might be voluntary and not forced" (Philem. 14). But he has already established that in his mind the request constitutes a duty not a favor.

It is not until verse 10 (40 percent of the way through the letter) that Paul gets to the point, saying, "I am appealing to you for my child Onesimus, whose father I have become during my imprisonment." Paul continues, "Formerly he was useless to you, but now he is useful both to you and to me" (Philem. 11). With this wordplay, Paul pivots the discussion from one about a bad slave to one about the common cause shared by Paul and Philemon—and now Onesimus as well. The conversation is not now about rights and wrongs but about effectiveness in the service of God and his purposes.

Food for Thought

Paul wants his friend to act out of love, not compunction. But his refusal to command Philemon still carries with it a large dose of pressure. What are some of those pressures?

Have you ever been obsessed with your own status and then someone else gave you a perspective that changed how you viewed the situation? What factors about their perspective led you to change your mind? Was it based in their authority over you? Or something beyond their rank and power?

_____

_____

_____

_____

_____

_____

_____

_____

Prayer

Dear God,

I have been both useless and useful in your work. Please lead me to find deep meaning and purpose as well as joy in obedience.

Amen.

Lesson #3: It's Personal in Every Direction

As Onesimus' legal owner, Philemon had the rank and power to punish Onesimus—even severely if he chose to do so. Paul, in his capacity as an apostle of the Lord, had the power to command Philemon to release Onesimus. The situation had all the makings of a stand-off—a power struggle. In Philemon's corner is social, economic, and legal power; in Paul's corner moral and spiritual status.

This struggle could quickly devolve into arguments about slavery, church and state, economics, social norms, personal property law, and all sorts of power plays. All of these arguments are beside the point that Paul wants to make. Moreover, they are counterproductive to the result he wants to achieve.

Instead of engaging in a power struggle, Paul diffuses the conflict by taking all aspects of rank and power off the table. Setting aside his own rank as an apostle, he sets the example—and perhaps the expectation—that Philemon will set aside his power as a slave owner in return. In any case, Paul recalibrates the discussion to be about relationships within the larger context of their mutual purpose. Both men serve Jesus Christ, their mutual master, and his kingdom. The first relationship—the prime mover of all other actions—is that of each man to his Lord and Savior.

In that context, each man is a brother to the other. And on that basis, Paul requests that Philemon welcome Onesimus (presumably to forgive him and forego any punishment), while at the same time requesting that Onesimus return voluntarily to Philemon. He asks both men to treat each other as brothers, rather than as slave and master.

Each of the three men in this story owes something to each of the others. Each of them has a claim over the others. Paul seeks to have all the debts and claims relinquished in favor of a mutual respect and service. Rather than dictating a solution to Philemon, Paul approaches him with respect, lays out a persuasive argument, and leaves the decision in Philemon's hands. Philemon could not have failed to notice Paul's clear desire, nor his statement that he would be following up with him (Philem. 21). But Paul manages the communication in an artful way that provides a model for resolving issues in the workplace.

Food for Thought

Paul's refocusing technique takes what could have been a complex battlefield and moves the discussion to a level playing field of shared value and purpose. How often and in what ways do you see productivity lost to personal rivalries between departments and employees? How can leaders shift focus from personal differences to shared values?

_____

_____

_____

_____

_____

_____

_____

The letter in this book is a communication between Paul and Philemon, but Paul has asked a big thing of Onesimus as well. Returning to Philemon carries a significant risk of punishment. It is easy to imagine that Paul had carried out a parallel discussion with the slave, asking him to return to Philemon in obedience to Jesus. Take a moment to construct an argument to persuade Onesimus to voluntarily return using Paul's arguments to Philemon as a model. How might this approach be used in your workplace?

_____

_____

_____

_____

_____

_____

_____

_____

Prayer

Father,

Teach me to love your ways and to obey you in all of mine. Help me to always seek your ways in resolving conflicts in my workplace.

Amen.

Chapter 2

Jesus Is a Leveler of Rank, Power, and Social Status

Lesson #1: From Slave to Brother to Apostle

Paul asks that Philemon not only welcome Onesimus back but that he receive the slave as if it were Paul himself returning. What a promotion. In a few sentences, Onesimus has gone from slave to brother to "apostle." Paul's reasoning is direct, "If you consider me a partner [*koinōnos*], receive him as you would me" (Philem. 17). Active fellowship means partnership. Paul has embraced the slave as a brother in Christ. For Philemon to do otherwise would be to break fellowship with Paul and uncouple the partnership.

Notice that there is no request that Philemon free Onesimus from his slave status. Only that, in the context of their shared faith in Christ, they be viewed as brothers—equals in the eyes of the Lord. As Paul wrote in Galatians 3:28, "There is neither Jew nor Gentile, neither slave nor free, nor is there male and female, for you are all one in Christ Jesus."

In Christ there is neither slave nor free, but in Paul's world, slavery is still an undeniable reality. Paul does not argue with this reality. Rather he gives this advice to believers:

> Were you a slave when you were called? Don't let it trouble you—although if you can gain your freedom, do so. For the one who was a slave when called to faith in the Lord is the Lord's freed person; similarly, the one who was free when called is Christ's

slave. You were bought at a price; do not become slaves of human beings. Brothers and sisters, each person, as responsible to God, should remain in the situation they were in when God called them. (1 Cor. 7:21–24 NIV)

The slave is free in Christ; the free man is Christ's slave. Regardless of a believer's station in life, all are equal in God's kingdom. That equality matters eternally. And yet it also has consequences in the present. In his letter to the Corinthians, Paul encourages the early Christians to work diligently and joyfully, even if their material situation doesn't change. Whether remaining in slavery or gaining freedom, workers can take courage from their assured identity as equals under God. This mentality makes work more joyful in the present moment, for leaders and subordinates alike.

Food for Thought

It's one thing to say that there is no master and slave in the eyes of God. It's another thing to have to live in our earthly reality. What difficulties arise in your workplace across lines of rank and power? What are ways that people of high or low status in the workplace can make relationships more comfortable and productive for all involved?

_____

_____

_____

_____

_____

_____

Leaders are frequently called to facilitate cross-functional projects. It is not uncommon for groups to have pre-established notions about others that are counterproductive to accomplishing your goals. Or perhaps you've seen people fall into hierarchical behaviors that stand in the way of progress. What steps can you take to encourage better communication?

_____

_____

_____

_____

_____

_____

_____

Prayer

Jesus,

I want to understand your ways and walk in them. Help me to see past the earthly obstacles to obey your commands fully and effectively. Equip me to direct others with your love and wisdom.

Amen.

Lesson #2: Brotherhood Is a Two-Way Street

In a gesture that parallels Paul's elevation of Onesimus' status from slave to brother, Paul sets aside his apostolic authority to appeal to Philemon as a prisoner or slave of Christ. The two images are flip sides of the same coin: since we all serve Jesus, any power, status, or rank we may have is relative and temporary. Writing in Ephesians, Paul counsels:

> Children, obey your parents in the Lord, for this is right. *Honor your father and mother* (which is the first commandment with a promise), *so that it may be well with you, and that you may live long on the earth.* Fathers, do not provoke your children to anger, but bring them up in the discipline and instruction of the Lord.
>
> Slaves, be obedient to those who are your masters according to the flesh, with fear and trembling, in the sincerity of your heart, as to Christ; not by way of eye service, as men-pleasers, but as slaves of Christ, doing the will of God from the heart. With good will render service, as to the Lord, and not to men, knowing that whatever good thing each one does, this he will receive back from the Lord, whether slave or free.
>
> And masters, do the same things to them, and give up threatening, knowing that both their Master and yours is in heaven, and there is no partiality with Him. (6:1–9 NASB)

According to this passage, we should do whatever work we do as if it's for God, serving him. This is as true for apostles and prophets as it is for the CEO, teacher, or table server. Because God values all people equally, he values the work each person does. This is especially true when that work is done "from the heart." This leveling of rank in the body of Christ goes in both directions. It reminds us that behind the rank the world gives us is our core humanity and shared identity in Christ.

Thus we are all the slaves Paul addresses when he writes,

Slaves, in all things obey those who are your masters on earth, not with external service, as those who merely please men, but with sincerity of heart, fearing the Lord. Whatever you do, do your work heartily, as for the Lord rather than for men, knowing that from the Lord you will receive the reward of the inheritance. It is the Lord Christ whom you serve. (Col. 3:18)

Food for Thought

In what ways does your position at work place demands on you to set an example? What behavior do you extend to those you work with that you would most like to receive in return?

_____

_____

_____

_____

_____

_____

Picture your workplace. If tomorrow you walked in and discovered that all titles were abolished, what would be the effect? Would work continue? Would you be able to manage effectively in the absence of direct authority? What role does rank play in your job?

_____

_____

_____

_____

Prayer

Father,

I know that we are all equal in your sight. Please send your Holy Spirit to impress the reality and comfort of this truth on my heart so that I might joyfully live it out in my workplace.

Amen.

Lesson #3: Specialized Functions in One Body with Many Members

Equal does not mean identical. In the body of Christ, it doesn't even mean similar. The kingdom of God, the profitable running of a business, and the productive management of a household all require excellence across a diverse set of functions. In Romans 12:3–8 (NASB), Paul says to every one of us:

> Do not think of yourself more highly than you ought, but rather think of yourself with sober judgment, in accordance with the faith God has distributed to each of you. For just as each of us has one body with many members, and these members do not all have the same function, so in Christ we, though many, form one body, and each member belongs to all the others. We have different gifts, according to the grace given to each of us. If your gift is prophesying, then prophesy in accordance with your faith; if it is serving, then serve; if it is teaching, then teach; if it is to encourage, then give encouragement; if it is giving, then give generously; if it is to lead, do it diligently; if it is to show mercy, do it cheerfully.

Differentiation in function and excellence in execution make any venture successful, whether it's a local church, a government, a school, or a commercial enterprise. As leaders, it is our job to identify the type of talents needed and then make it easy for people to perform well.

Paul recognizes that Onesimus had a talent for helpfulness. This talent extends past Onesimus' role as a slave, and Paul is eager to put it to use for the good of the wider Christian community. In this way Paul is acting as a future-minded manager, noticing and nurturing potential when he discovers it. Paul also remarks on Philemon's particular talent for loving other Christians (Philem. 5). Paul hopes Philemon will extend his talent to loving Onesimus as a brother, and thus diffuse a potentially explosive situation in the early Christian community. This is also savvy leadership on the part of Paul. He anticipates Philemon's objection to taking Onesimus back by demonstrating that it's already within Philemon's core competency.

Food for Thought

God clearly delights in diversity. His creation is artfully formed and equipped for specific functions. Yet in many modern cultures, there is a tendency to equate difference with injustice, as different functions can command different earnings. Think of your workplace. What are some examples of good diversity and bad disparities?

_____

_____

_____

_____

In order to set up Onesimus and Philemon for a good outcome, Paul praises their individual talents. Think of the people you work with every day. What are their special talents? Is there some way you can praise them today?

Prayer

Father,

I ask that you teach me how to translate your perspective into my daily work. I pray for those people who work for me that I honor and encourage their talents.

Amen.

Chapter 3

Leadership Is Grounded in Relationships

Lesson #1: Relationships at Work

Leadership, as modeled by Paul, is not about the exercise of power, status, or even efficiency. His leadership is grounded in relationships. Paul uses a participatory style of leadership that draws others into his decision making. Paul ultimately asks Philemon to acknowledge Onesimus' newness in Jesus. But Paul does so by first pointing out his existing relationship with Philemon, which he strengthens by praising Philemon's virtues and judgment. The name "Philemon" means "affectionate" in Greek (literally, "who kisses"). It is this virtue that Paul tries to draw out of Philemon with his praise. This tactic serves to strengthen Paul's relationship with Philemon, while forging a new relationship between Philemon and Onesimus.

From the opening pages of the Bible, in Genesis 1:26–27, we see God as a God of relationships:

> Then God said, "Let us make man in our image, after our likeness. And let them have dominion over the fish of the sea and over the birds of the heavens and over the livestock and over all the earth and over every creeping thing that creeps on the earth." So God created man in his own image, in the image of God he created him; male and female he created them.

God is inherently relational. Within the created universe, God is present in relationship with his creatures and especially with people. Laboring in God's image, we work in creation, on creation, with creation and—if we work as God intends—for creation.

Relationships are a huge part of work. First, there are so many of them. We deal with executives, co-workers, customers, vendors, and those under our authority—asynchronously, on-demand, and simultaneously. Often these relationships are with people we might not ordinarily choose to spend time with.

Second, these relationships exist under the pressure of deadlines, performance goals, and competition, which can stress connections over extended periods of time. The time we spend in the workplace and the intensity of our work make it a natural breeding ground for great friendships and animosity alike.

The leader is responsible for establishing an environment, to the best of their ability, in which healthy relationships can flourish for the good of both the individuals and the organization itself. Doing so is a high-stakes balancing act of priorities, prayer, knowledge of individual personalities, and creating shared goals. Paul uses his leadership to forge a better relationship between Philemon and Onesimus, one that honors their individual personalities and unites them through their shared goal of serving Christ.

Food for Thought

What difference does it make that we are bearers of the divine image in our work? How do you reflect God's image as a leader? In your interactions at work, how can you increasingly look for, encourage, and honor the image of God in others?

_____

_____

_____

_____

_____

_____

Christians are called to reflect God's own virtues of "compassion, kindness, humility, meekness and patience" (Col. 3:12) in whatever we do. In what ways is this concept either harder or easier to put into action for those in leadership?

_____

_____

_____

_____

_____

_____

Prayer

Dear God,

I know that you are a God of relationships. Too often I put the immediacy of work objectives above the superior value of relationships. Please strengthen my resolve and soften my heart to serve all those around me every day.

Amen.

Lesson #2: Image-Bearers at Work

Jesus underscores the importance of relationships when he says, "So if you are offering your gift at the altar and there remember that your brother has something against you, leave your gift there before the altar and go. First be reconciled to your brother, and then come and offer your gift" (Matt. 5:23–24). Our relationship with others is directly tied to our relationship with God. Clearly God intends that we have a sense of urgency in resolving things when they get broken.

In Colossians 3:13, Paul exhorts us to "put up with one another," frequently translated to read "bear with one another." Although "bear with one another" has a lofty ring to it, the phrase doesn't fully capture Paul's point. He recognizes that there are all kinds of people in the church and in our workplaces who just aren't people we naturally enjoy. Our interests and personalities are so different that there is no natural point of connection. But we put up with them anyway, and they put up with us.

We seek their good, we forgive their sins, and we endure their irritating idiosyncrasies. In fact, many of the character traits Paul extols in his letters can be summarized in the phrase, "That person works well with others." Paul frequently mentions such people by name including Onesimus in Colossian 4:9.

For the Christian leader, being a "team player" is not merely cliché. It is a foundational Christian virtue. Christians are meant to show the new life of Christ to those around them. The workplace is arguably the best forum for trying out what Christ-inspired putting up with one another might look like.

Paul's exhortation is to work toward good relationships, especially at work. This means directly confronting people who have wronged us, instead of gossiping about them behind their backs (Matt. 18:15–17). It means working to correct inequities in the workplace and forgiving those who cause them to occur. It means speaking the truth in love and in deed, integrating our life in Christ with our life at work. It means praying specifically for the work we are in the midst of doing. We can imagine a lawyer asking, "God, please show me how to respect both the plaintiff and the defendant in the language I use in this brief. I forgive the opposing counsel. Let me say only what is true and just in your eyes."

Food for Thought

We represent Jesus in the workplace. As Christ-followers, how we treat others and how diligently and faithfully we do our work reflects on our Lord. How well do your actions reflect him? Do you find it easier—more natural—to represent Jesus when you are dealing with peers, subordinates, superiors, or those outside your organization? If so, why?

_____

_____

_____

_____

Like the lawyer who works for one side, but wants to show respect for all, most leaders find themselves managing multiple, conflicting interests. What are some of the conflicting demands you face? Write down some ideas to pray about them.

Prayer

Jesus,

Thank you for making your priorities so clear to us. I ask that your priorities be mine in my heart, soul, and mind, to your glory in my workplace.

Amen.

Lesson #3: Technology and Relationships

The apostle John, who like Paul was an influential leader in the early Christian church, ends his second letter by saying that he wants to continue the conversation in person. "Although I have much to write to you, I would rather not use paper and ink. Instead I hope to come to you and talk with you face to face" (2 John 1:12). Perhaps he realizes that whatever else he has to communicate could be misunderstood if presented in the impersonal medium of a letter. When it comes to sensitive communications, some things are better said in person. This is true even if distance makes it difficult to see one another face to face. Leadership beyond rank and power includes finding ways of communication that improve relationships rather than simply conveying information and instructions.

How does technology affect relationships at work? In twenty-first-century workplaces we find complex challenges with personal communication. Because of the speed of business and the geographic distribution of organizations, many of our communications at work are carried out electronically. And among electronic communications there are so many options. Choices include video conferencing, telephone, texting, e-mail, social media, and proprietary workflow management systems. But effective communication still requires matching the medium to the nature of the message. E-mail might be the most effective medium for placing an order, but it's probably not best for communicating a performance review. The more complicated or emotionally charged the message, the more immediate and personal the medium needs to be.

The challenge of what to say in writing and what to say face to face is not a new one. In 2 Corinthians 2:3 (NIV) Paul writes, "I wrote as I did so that when I came I should not be distressed by those who ought to make me rejoice."

Physical presence offers the best opportunity for building trust (which is essential for any team) and dealing with nuance. It isn't just the formal meeting that counts here, but the side conversations that establish deeper relationships. The strongest relationships typically start with physical presence, cycling back to that to prevent the relationship lag that develops when people don't know each other well or when they drift apart. Group communication, such as through video and telephone conferencing, can be helpful in clarifying objectives and gaining agreement. The important thing we learn from the letters of Paul and John is that the value of relationships is paramount, and the best method of communication is one that honors those relationships.

Food for Thought

In a 2010 interview with Ethix.org, Pat Gelsinger, once senior vice president of Intel, discussed how he deals with the challenges of technology mediated communication: "I have a personal rule. If I go back and forth with somebody in email more than four or five times on the same topic, I stop. No more. We get on the phone, or we get together face to face." Can you think of times that the choice of communication vehicle either helped or hurt you in your work?

_____

_____

_____

_____

_____

_____

When it comes to relationships, we need to make wise choices about the role of technology in our communications. How do you model your values through your communication practices?

_____

_____

_____

_____

_____

_____

_____

_____

Prayer

God,

Too often I sacrifice human touch for the expediency of technology. Help me to be more aware.

Amen.

Chapter 4
Leadership in Action

Lesson #1: Leaders Grow People

Good leaders help other people develop by teaching them how to make sound choices. This is in contrast to authoritarian leaders who command other people to do things without thinking. Paul, as a leader, is not just looking for Philemon to obey a command. Rather, Paul wants Philemon to make the right decision with a clear understanding of what makes it a good decision. He appeals to Philemon's free will so that Philemon can be responsible for his own character and values. There is a folk truism that says, "He who is convinced against his will is of the same opinion still." Any act that comes from compulsion is a one-off. Once the compulsion is removed, the behavior reverts back to where it had been before, and there is no gain for character. Paul wants Philemon to act from his own heart and grow because of it.

Now of course that doesn't mean Paul doesn't try to influence Philemon's decision. Far from it. Paul places great moral pressure and even some social pressure on Philemon as well. Paul is not subtle in his stance. Paul reminds Philemon of the debt he has to Paul: "So if you consider me your partner, welcome him as you would welcome me" (Philem. 17).

Yet at the same time Paul mentors Philemon, who is himself a church leader, by modeling the behavior he wants to see. In two small verses Paul models both love for Onesimus (the very thing he wants to cultivate in Philemon) and relinquishing control over others (something that might be difficult for a slave owner).

> I am sending him back to you, sending my very heart. I would have been glad to keep him with me, in order that he might serve me on your behalf during my imprisonment for the gospel, but I preferred to do nothing without your consent in order that your goodness might not be by compulsion but of your own accord.
> (Philem. 12–14)

When we lead as Paul does, with a concern for building character, when we are willing to see potential and create space for growth and change in another, and when we are willing to sacrifice in the process, we are serving God in our leadership. Godly leaders guide others into being better, not only in the tasks they perform but in how they do them. When these lessons occur within loving relationships, this is what Paul calls real fellowship.

Food for Thought

Think of a good leader you know personally. How has this person helped others to grow? What lessons has this person taught you, and how did he or she teach them?

_____

_____

_____

_____

_____

_____

_____

Are there specific character traits you would like to see developed in the people with whom you work? How are you modeling those traits now? How could you impart a clearer lesson?

_____

_____

_____

_____

_____

_____

_____

_____

Prayer

Jesus,

Thank you for the unimaginable mercy you have extended to me. I ask your Holy Spirit to grow in me compassion and mercy so that I may help those around me to flourish.

Amen.

Lesson #2: Leaders Exert Authority

The fact that Paul elected not to exercise his authority in the matter of Philemon and Onesimus cannot be confused with an inability to do so. Quite the opposite is true. Paul publicly, precisely, and vehemently chastised the apostle Peter for hypocrisy, misleading the people, and misrepresenting Christ:

> When Cephas [Peter] came to Antioch, I opposed him to his face, because he stood condemned. For before certain men came from James, he used to eat with the Gentiles. But when they arrived, he began to draw back and separate himself from the Gentiles because he was afraid of those who belonged to the circumcision group. The other Jews joined him in his hypocrisy, so that by their hypocrisy even Barnabas was led astray.
>
> When I saw that they were not acting in line with the truth of the gospel, I said to Cephas in front of them all, "You are a Jew, yet you live like a Gentile and not like a Jew. How is it, then, that you force Gentiles to follow Jewish customs? We who are Jews by birth and not sinful Gentiles know that a person is not justified by the works of the law, but by faith in Jesus Christ. So we, too, have put our faith in Christ Jesus that we may be justified by faith in Christ and not by the works of the law, because by the works of the law no one will be justified. But if, in seeking to be justified in Christ, we Jews find ourselves also among the sinners, doesn't that mean that Christ promotes sin? Absolutely not! If I rebuild what I destroyed, then I really would be a lawbreaker. (Gal. 2:11–17)

That Peter had behaved in a spineless manner might have been an occasion to take him aside for a private rebuke as recommended in Matthew 18:15–18 for conflict resolution. But Peter—arguably foremost of the leaders in the newly forming church—had been very public in his misdeed. The matter had to be resolved publicly. Paul acted as a leader, decisively rebuking Peter to set straight the false teaching his actions implied.

Paul concludes his explanation by saying, "I have been crucified with Christ and I no longer live, but Christ lives in me (Gal. 2:19–20). Leaders have to be able to recognize when it is time to exercise authority, even if it might be uncomfortable to do so. Christian leaders have the comfort of knowing that Christ is alive in them, with spiritual authority as well as with mercy.

Food for Thought

There is a wise saying that admonishes, "Don't mistake kindness for weakness." How does your workplace view the exercise of power? What kind of balance do you see at work? What is your comfort and skill level with using your own authority?

_____
_____
_____
_____
_____
_____

Paul's public admonition put him in direct conflict with Peter, but there is no evidence that their relationship was damaged. It is likely that Peter knew the truth when he heard it. Have you ever been on the receiving end of a rebuke like this one? How did you react?

_____
_____
_____
_____
_____
_____

Prayer

Father God,

I ask that you equip me to exercise authority in love and to accept rebuke with gratitude.

Amen.

Lesson #3: Leaders Bear the Cost

Leaders take accountability for their actions and share the cost of consequences. When Paul made his request of Philemon, he acknowledged the possibility that Onesimus' actions may well have resulted in costs. He asks that such costs be reckoned to his own account. Paul will cover any damages Onesimus owes. He even writes this offer in his own hand to make the point as personally as possible.

As a leader, Paul is willing to bear the cost of the sacrifices he asks others to make. This offer creates a sense of justice and balance as he asks for leniency and compassion. This bearing another's burden is part of the active participation of fellowship that Paul promotes in this letter. By injecting himself into the relational equation, Paul also makes himself a participant in this situation, becoming part of the fellowship he calls Philemon to display.

A visitor to the Theology of Work website (www.theologyofwork.org) told the following story in a comment on the Philemon and Colossians commentary:

> I had a friend in Special Forces who was training a team of Afghani locals out in the desert. It was so hot they could only travel by night. He became aware of a desperate man who had lost his papers in the desert and was facing three days in jail as well as

a physical lashing. My friend ordered the man into the shelter telling him, "I will find your papers." He layered up, and began backtracking their steps into the desert in 120-degree heat. Two hours later, he returned the papers to the man.

The man was overwhelmed, and asked why my friend did such a thing. My friend replied that this was how God had treated him in Jesus Christ, and reflected how God feels about us. My friend took on the burden of dehydration and heat exhaustion. Sick for hours, he took the burden of the man's debt upon himself in an effort to personally remove the sentence from the man. He suffered in his place. Nothing speaks louder than that.

Food for Thought

In the workplace, we don't simply model Christ by taking the position of forgiveness Paul is requesting of Philemon. That's one aspect, but we fully embody the cross when we model Paul himself, and offer to absorb the debt ourselves. What are some ways, as a manager, that you can absorb grievances that co-workers have against each other?

_____

_____

_____

_____

_____

_____

_____

The debt Paul is willing to bear mirrors the parable Jesus told of the Good Samaritan (Luke 10:25–37). Not only did the Samaritan rescue the man beaten up on the side of the road, but paid the innkeeper for any debt the injured man might incur during his recovery at the inn. Think of some ways you can actively promote such "cost sharing" in your workplace. What impact might this have?

_____

_____

_____

_____

_____

_____

_____

Prayer

Jesus,

Help me embody the ministry of reconciliation at work. Just as you absorbed the debt I carried and made peace between myself and God, help me to reflect your glory as I mirror your grace.

Amen.

Chapter 5

Leadership Is Service

Lesson #1: Leaders Are Servants

When Paul put aside his rank and authority over Philemon, he gave his friend the chance to do the right thing and grow as a leader. This action is consistent with many of his statements across the Epistles, especially, "Follow my example, as I follow the example of Christ" (1 Cor. 1:11). We will not be called upon to raise the dead, change water to wine, or die to redeem creation. But we are called to follow Jesus' example in the way we serve others.

In Mark 10, Jesus speaks passionately to his disciples about his approaching death. Without missing a beat, brothers James and John ask Jesus for prime positions in his new kingdom—a request that angers the other ten (most likely because the brothers had taken a first-movers advantage than because the request was callous and self-absorbed). At this point,

> Jesus called them together and said, "You know that those who are regarded as rulers of the Gentiles lord it over them, and their high officials exercise authority over them. Not so with you. Instead, whoever wants to become great among you must be your servant, and whoever wants to be first must be slave of all. For even the Son of Man did not come to be served, but to serve, and to give his life as a ransom for many." (Mark 10:42–45 NIV)

Jesus gave a visual picture of the fact that he came to serve when he wrapped a towel around his waist and bent to wash the feet of his disciples. Jesus explicitly tells them—and by extension us—that we are to follow his example. "So if I, your Lord and Teacher, have washed your feet, you also ought to wash one another's feet. For I have set you an example" (John 13:14–15).

This attitude of humble service should accompany all we do. If the CEO walks a production floor, it should be as if coming to wash the assembly workers' feet. So, too, the gas station attendant should clean the bathroom floors as if they were his customers' feet. Jesus, the Spirit-filled teacher who reigns over the entire cosmos, both dignifies and demands humble acts of service from his followers because godly work is done for the benefit of others, not merely for the fulfillment of ourselves.

Food for Thought

Al Cardonne CEO of Cardonne Industries said in an interview, "My employees are my customers. When I treat them right they treat the company's customers right too. Work is worship." How does the idea that leaders are servants elevate work into a form of worship?

Washing feet was a real task for servants of Jesus' day, serving a practical purpose that is not needed in much of the world today. What are some practical equivalents of foot washing in your workplace today? What might you accomplish by performing them? What reactions would you expect from others?

_____

_____

_____

_____

_____

_____

_____

Prayer

Jesus,

You made the need to serve others so clear in your life, death, and resurrection. Teach me to always look for ways to serve others.

Amen.

Lesson #2: Leaders in Service

Paul offers a definitive statement of what it means to be a leader when he says, "Think of us in this way, as servants of Christ and stewards of God's mysteries" (1 Cor. 4:1). Although "us" refers to the apostolic leaders, it applies also to leaders today who consider themselves servants of that foot-washing Savior.

Paul uses two words in this verse to elaborate what he means. The first, *hypēretēs* ("servants"), denotes an attendant, a servant who waits on or assists others. In this sense, leaders attend personally to the needs of the people they lead. Leaders are not exalted, but humbled, by accepting a job that requires patience, personal engagement, and individual attention to the needs of their followers.

The second is *oikonomos* ("stewards"), which describes a servant or slave who manages the affairs of a household or estate. The chief distinction in this position is trust. The steward is trusted to manage the affairs of the household for the benefit of the owner. Likewise, the leader is trusted to manage a group for the benefit of all its members, rather than for the leader's personal benefit. As a servant and a steward, the leader performs personalized service for the benefit of others, executed in trust.

Service, not greatness, is the Christian's purpose. Paul's statement, "We do not proclaim ourselves; we proclaim Jesus Christ as Lord and ourselves as your slaves for Jesus' sake" (2 Cor. 4:5) is one of the classic biblical examples of the concept that has come to be known as "servant leadership." Paul, the foremost leader of the Christian movement beyond the confines of Palestine, calls himself "your slave for Jesus' sake."

This fundamentally Christian insight should inform our attitude in any leadership position. Servant leadership does not mean that we refrain from exercising legitimate authority or that we lead timidly. The opposite is true—we owe outstanding performance to our organizations. It means that, in our pursuit of excellent outcomes, we use our position and our power to further others' well-being before our own.

Food for Thought

Paul calls himself a slave "for Jesus' sake." A slave, as Jesus pointed out, works all day in the fields, then comes in and serves dinner to the household, and only afterwards eats and drinks himself (Luke 17:7–10). Does this mean that as Christians, we should not accept leadership positions unless we intend to sacrifice the privilege of taking care of ourselves before taking care of others?

_____

_____

_____

_____

_____

_____

Paul suffered affliction, perplexity, and persecution nearly to the point of death (2 Cor. 4:8–12). Have you suffered for serving others? Is suffering a necessary part of leadership?

_____

_____

_____

_____

_____

_____

Prayer

Dear Lord,

I am challenged by your vision of servant leadership. Transform my thinking and my attitudes that I may lift up those who are officially below me, seeking to honor them and acknowledge their contributions. Help me to exercise the authority given to me with humility, always seeing myself first and foremost as your servant, and therefore the servant of others.

Amen.

Lesson #3: Leaders Trust God's Provision

The concept of servant leadership is timeless. Although the modern term was coined by Robert Greenleaf in 1970, the spirit of servant leadership can be found in the Tao Te Ching, attributed to Lao-Tzu who lived in China as early as 570 BC, when he said, "The highest type of ruler is one whose existence the people are barely aware." But it reaches its highest and most natural expression in the life of the believing leader who prayerfully and effectively serves others in imitation of Christ.

In Philippians 2:3–4 (NIV), we are told, "Do nothing out of selfish ambition or vain conceit. Rather, in humility value others above yourselves, not looking to your own interests but each of you to the interests of the others." This is a sentiment that secular proponents of servant leadership would agree with. But the Christian model of servant leadership parts company with Greenleaf and Lao-Tzu with the urgent motivation for servant leadership captured in Philippians 2:5–8:

> In your relationships with one another, have the same mindset as Christ Jesus: Who, being in very nature God, did not consider

equality with God something to be used to his own advantage; rather, he made himself nothing by taking the very nature of a servant, being made in human likeness. And being found in appearance as a man, he humbled himself by becoming obedient to death—even death on a cross!

For the believer, servant leadership is not merely a leadership style but a lifelong mandate based on grace.

Following Christ makes us able to trust God for our provision, which in turn leads us to confidently work for the benefit of others in need. The most powerful measure of our trust in God is not what we do for ourselves but what we do for others. When we work for God, we serve others—equipping them to succeed and remaining committed to their success. When we serve others, we bring God's blessing into a fallen world and honor to the one who loved us first.

Food for Thought

We can assess our level of trust in God's provision by examining the things we do to provide for ourselves. At work, do we hoard knowledge to make ourselves indispensable? Do we require employment contracts or golden parachutes to feel secure in our future? What does the pattern of what you do at work say about your degree of trust in God's provision?

_____

_____

_____

_____

_____

_____

When a leader trusts God they help others to do well at work without counting the cost or risk to themselves. Do we risk our positions to stand up for our co-workers, customers, suppliers, and others who are powerless or in need? Do we choose—within whatever scope of choice we may have—to work in ways that benefit others in need, as much as ways that benefit ourselves?

Prayer

Father,

It is so challenging and humbling to have the honor of serving your purposes in my work. When I think of all that Jesus has done for me and how little you ask in return, I am so sorry for my uneven efforts. Ignite my heart to serve everyone in my workplace with a passion and joy that accurately reflects my Lord and my Savior, Jesus Christ.

Amen.

Chapter 6

Leadership in Difficult Times

Lesson #1: Leaders Face Opposition

One of the best leaders across time was Moses, whose life exemplifies almost every challenge, reward, quality, and consequence of leadership. From the beginning of the book of Exodus to the end of Deuteronomy, the figure of Moses dominates the history of the Jewish people. Three episodes from the book of Numbers illustrate Moses' godly leadership in difficult times.

In Numbers 12, Moses' brother and sister, Aaron and Miriam, launch a revolt against his authority. God punishes them swiftly and severely on Moses' behalf. He reminds them that he has chosen Moses as his representative to Israel, speaking "face to face" with Moses (Num. 12:7–8). He asks, "Why then were you not afraid to speak against my servant Moses?" (Num. 12:8). When he hears no answer, Numbers tells us that "the anger of the Lord was kindled against them" (Num. 12:9).

Although Moses was both powerful and in the right, he responds to the leadership challenge with gentleness and humility. "The man Moses was very humble, more so than anyone else on the face of the earth" (Num. 12:3). He remains with Aaron and Miriam successfully intervening with God to restore Miriam's health (Num. 12:13–15), and he retains them in senior leadership of the nation.

In positions of authority, we are likely to face opposition. We have a right to defend our position against those who are attacking it.

Yet, like Moses, we must care first for the people over whom God has placed us in authority, including those who are opposing us. We look for common ground, or we may find it impossible to restore good working relationships. But in every leadership situation we have the duty of godly humility. This duty means that we act for the good of those God has entrusted to us, even at the expense of our comfort, power, prestige, and self-image.

Food for Thought

God was uniquely present in Moses' life. "Never since then has there arisen a prophet in Israel like Moses, whom the Lord knew face to face" (Deut. 34:10). Today's leaders do not manifest God's authority face to face as Moses did. Yet God commands us to respect the authority of all leaders, "for there is no authority except from God" (Rom. 13:1–3). In the workplace, passive-aggressive measures, back-stabbing, and gossip are all too common responses to bad management. What are legitimate, productive, and godly ways to challenge leaders?

Inherent in Moses' treatment of these rebels is forgiveness and the humility to extend forgiveness passionately. He also demonstrated wisdom in retaining the chastened leaders, as well as a selfless regard for the well-being of his people. When you are wronged in the workplace, especially by subordinates, what is your gut reaction? What is your reasoned response? How do you demonstrate forgiveness when it is appropriate?

Prayer

Father,

I come to you to ask for your forgiveness for the times I have reacted to challenge defensively. Open my heart to forgive with the forgiveness I have received from you and to restore those who have been wounded by their own actions.

Amen.

Lesson #2: Leaders Stay the Course

Another challenge to Moses' authority arises in Numbers 13 and 14. The Lord tells Moses to send spies into the land of Canaan to prepare for the conquest. Both military and economic intelligence are to be collected, and spies are named from every tribe (Num. 13:18–20). The spies' report good news and bad news: the land is very good, so good "it flows with milk and honey" (Num. 13:27), but "the people who live in the land are strong, and the towns are fortified and very large" (Num. 13:28). Full of fear, the spies—effectively representing all of Israel—declare that the land cannot be conquered (Num. 13:30–32). The people resolve to find a new leader to take them back to slavery in Egypt. Only Aaron, Caleb, and a young man named Joshua remain with Moses.

Moses stands firm, despite the plan's unpopularity. Although his people are on the verge of replacing him, he stays the course following what the Lord had revealed to him as right. He and Aaron plead with the people to cease their rebellion, to no avail. In response to the rebellion—rejection of God's plan—the Lord strikes the people with a deadly pestilence (Num. 14:5–12). Moses intervenes for them, appealing to the Lord to forgive the people and save them from complete destruction. The Lord relents, but declares there will be inescapable consequences nonetheless. None of those who joined the rebellion will be allowed to enter the Promised Land (Num. 14:20–23).

Leadership can be a lonely duty, tempting us to bend to popular opinion. Moses' actions exemplify the responsibility of leaders to act with decisive commitment regardless of the prevailing winds of opinion. While it is true that good leaders do listen to others' opinions, they do so to inform their decision making, not to be persuaded to act against sound judgment. When leaders know the best course of action, and have tested that knowledge to the best of their ability, those leaders have a responsibility to do what is best, not what is most popular, easiest, or most comfortable.

🍲 *Food for Thought*

In Moses' situation, there was no doubt about the right course of action. The Lord had commanded Moses to occupy the Promised Land. Moses remained humble, but he did not waver. And yet, he did not succeed in carrying out the Lord's command. After all, if people will not follow a leader, the mission fails. In this case, the consequence for the people was that an entire generation missed out on the land God had chosen for them. Have you ever been in a situation where you needed to stay an unpopular course? How can you lead others to follow you in such a situation?

_____

_____

_____

_____

_____

_____

_____

Abraham Lincoln became one of America's greatest presidents by steadfastly refusing to give in to popular opinion to end the American Civil War by accepting the nation's division. Although he had the humility to acknowledge the possibility that he might be wrong ("as God gives us to see the right"), he also had the fortitude to do what he knew was right despite enormous pressure to give in. There is a difference between being proudly stubborn and humbly stable. How can we be sure of our motivations in such circumstances?

___

Prayer

Dear God,

Thank you for increasing my grasp of my responsibilities as a leader. It is my deep desire to honor you in service to everyone in my workplace. I ask for wisdom and generosity in time of conflict.

Amen.

Lesson #3: Leaders Fail

Moses' moment of failure came when the people of Israel resumed their complaints about food and water (Num. 20:1–5). Moses and Aaron brought the complaint to the Lord, who told them to take their staff, and in the people's presence command a rock to yield water enough for the people and their livestock

(Num. 20:6–8). Moses did as the Lord instructed but added two flourishes of his own. First he rebuked the people, saying, "Listen, you rebels, shall we bring water for you out of this rock?" Then he struck the rock twice with his staff. Water poured out in abundance (Num. 20:9–11), but the Lord was extremely displeased with Moses and Aaron.

God's punishment was harsh. "Because you did not trust in me, to show my holiness before the eyes of the Israelites, therefore you shall not bring this assembly into the land that I have given them" (Num.20:12). Moses and Aaron, like all the people who rebelled against God's plan earlier (Num. 14:22–23), would not be permitted to enter the Promised Land. Numbers 20:12 names Moses' offense directly, "You did not trust in me." Moses' leadership faltered in the crucial moment when he stopped trusting God and started acting on his own impulses.

By God's grace, even failure as great as Moses' at Meribah—failures with disastrous consequences in this life—do not separate us from the ultimate fulfillment of God's promises. Moses did not enter the Promised Land, but God graciously let him see the full extent of the land before he died. Deuteronomy 34:6 tells us that God himself buried Moses' body. And the New Testament declares Moses "faithful in all God's house" (Heb. 3:2–6). Thus nothing can separate us from the love of God, not even human failure.

Honoring God in leadership is a humbling responsibility, whether we lead a global enterprise, a classroom, or a relief organization. We run the risk of mistaking our authority for God's. Meeting regularly with an accountability or peer group, praying daily about the tasks of leadership, keeping a weekly Sabbath to rest in God's presence, and seeking others' perspective on God's guidance are some things we can do to stay aligned with God. But there is no substitute for trusting God and remaining wholly dependent on him. Moses' failure stands as a warning of our own vulnerabilities, and as an encouragement that there is loving forgiveness even in the presence of the consequences of failure.

Food for Thought

God tells us that his grace is sufficient for us. What fears threaten to chip away at your trust in God in your workplace? How can you hold the sufficiency of God's grace as a central motivating factor in your job?

Prayer

Father God,

You lovingly and personally tended to Moses' body at the end of his life. Thank you for showing yourself to be all righteous and all giving. And most of all, thank you for the gift of your grace.

Amen.

Chapter 7
The Impact of Leadership

Lesson #1: Leaders Bring Good and Evil

Deuteronomy ends with Moses' death and the transition of leadership to Joshua (Deut. 34:9). It becomes Joshua's job to lead Israel into the land of promise. Under his leadership, the Israelites did work to possess the land, but they did not do it thoroughly. If the work of Israel was to possess the land and to obey God by completely eradicating the people and goods in the promised territory, they didn't do a great job. The ramifications of that poor workmanship become obvious in the book of Judges.

The narrative flow through Joshua and Judges demonstrates the absolute impact leaders have on the effectiveness of a group—for good or for evil. God, working with and through Moses had established a people, and by Joshua he established a land. From these stories we see that the effect of good leadership lasts about a generation, "Israel served the Lord throughout the lifetime of Joshua and of the elders who outlived him and who had experienced everything the Lord had done for Israel" (Josh. 24:31).

In Judges, the good effect of Joshua's leadership completely dissipates:

> After that whole generation had been gathered to their ancestors, another generation grew up who knew neither the Lord nor what he had done for Israel. Then the Israelites did evil in the eyes of the Lord and served the Baals. They forsook the Lord, the God

of their ancestors, who had brought them out of Egypt. They followed and worshiped various gods of the peoples around them.
(Judg. 2:10–12 NIV)

We are told repeatedly that "In those days Israel had no king; everyone did as they saw fit" (Judg. 17:6)—and we are shown repeatedly just how bad that approach is for an individual or a nation. So begins the repeated cycle of Judges,

> Whenever the Lord raised up a judge for them, he was with the judge and saved them out of the hands of their enemies as long as the judge lived; for the Lord relented because of their groaning under those who oppressed and afflicted them. But when the judge died, the people returned to ways even more corrupt than those of their ancestors, following other gods and serving and worshiping them. They refused to give up their evil practices and stubborn ways. (Judg. 2:18–19 NIV)

Leadership directly impacts outcomes for good or for bad—changing lives along the way.

Food for Thought

Throughout the book of Judges, when the misery level rises high enough for the people to repent, God answers their pleas with good leaders. Take a moment to think of the impact you have on different individuals and groups of people in your workplace. Can you see yourself as a gift from God to the people under your care? You may be an answer to prayer.

_____

_____

_____

_____

We often find ourselves drifting away from God as we decide how to handle the many opportunities and challenges that arise in our work. We discover that we have elevated other concerns above loving and serving him through our work. The message of Joshua and Judges is that God is ready for us to return to him and receive his blessings in our life and work.

Prayer

> *Jesus,*
>
> *Help me to follow you completely with joy and passion instead of doing whatever I think is fit.*
>
> *Amen.*

Lesson #2: Leaders Build Leaders

Building a sustainable organization—in this case, the nation of Israel—requires the orderly transition of authority. Without continuity, people become confused and fearful, work structures fall apart, and workers become ineffective, like sheep without a shepherd. Preparing a successor takes time and investment on the part of the mentoring leader. Poor leaders may be afraid to equip someone capable of succeeding them, but great leaders like Moses begin developing successors long before they expect to leave office. And they are not afraid to share their power. Moses made sure to very publicly recognize and support Joshua to confirm his authority in front of all Israel (Num. 27:17–21).

Under the tutelage of Moses and the grace of God, Joshua became a great leader who not only brought Israel into the Promised Land, but whose godly influence was strong enough to sustain a generation after his death. Was he a born leader? Probably not. We read that Joshua had to be told—repeatedly by Moses, by God, and even by the Reubenites, the Gadites, and the half-tribe of Manasseh—to be strong and courageous. Why would everyone have to tell Joshua to be strong and courageous if he were a natural?

Joshua wasn't a coward; he was first and foremost a gifted military leader. But he wasn't yet a commander-in-chief capable of leading the complex nation of Israel. In Numbers 13:16, Moses changes this military leader's name from Hoshea ("salvation") to Joshua ("the Lord saves")—a fitting transition from a functional military leader/manager to an executive responsible for the spiritual, physical, and civic well-being of a nation. Joshua moves through his executive training under Moses while demonstrating faithfulness, trustworthiness, obedience, loyalty, humility, a teachable spirit, godliness, and a willing heart.

As an example to today's leaders, Joshua's most notable characteristic may be his willingness to keep growing in virtue throughout his life. Unlike Samson, who seems stuck in infantile willfulness, Joshua transitions from a hot-blooded young man (Num. 14:6–10) to a military commander (Josh. 6:1–21) to a national chief executive (Josh. 20) and eventually to a prophetic visionary (Josh. 24). He is more than willing to subject himself to a long period of training under Moses and to learn from those more experienced than him. He never seems to refuse an opportunity to grow in character or to benefit from the wisdom of others.

Food for Thought

Moses mentored Joshua very successfully. The book of Joshua watches this novice executive grow in excellence as he moves from being introduced in Joshua 1:1 as, "Joshua son of Nun, Moses' aide" to "Joshua son of Nun, the servant of the Lord" at his burial (Josh. 24:29). God's work is not done at Joshua's death. But Joshua's work is done and all of God's promises have been kept. What would your workplace be like without you? Are you equipping others to continue your work in your absence?

_____

_____

_____

_____

_____

_____

_____

Do you have an accurate view of your strengths as well as your weaknesses? How can you be strong and courageous as well as at peace with your short comings?

_____

_____

_____

_____

_____

_____

_____

Prayer

Holy Spirit,

I ask that you work in me to develop an increasingly teachable spirit and an effectively generous ability to build up others in my workplace. Please protect others from my shortcomings as you mold me into your servant.

Amen.

Lesson #3: Leaders Resolve Conflicts

Paul worked skillfully to help resolve the conflict between Philemon and Onesimus, using every resource available, other than direct, authoritarian command. Because conflict is a part of everyday life, good leaders learn to craft solutions that turn conflicts into resolutions—and, like Paul, they use every resource in their arsenal.

Similarly, Ken Melrose, CEO of Toro, manufacturer of high quality lawnmowers took an innovative approach using legal, engineering, and customer service resources to set a new standard for customer service. Like all lawnmower makers, Toro faced lawsuits from consumers who had injured themselves by using the mower improperly. Ken Melrose, a Christian, believed the company's adversarial legal stance was inconsistent with the great customer service it strove to give in every other situation. He reframed the question as, "How could the company serve people injured when using its products, yet protect itself against frivolous lawsuits and excessive demands for compensation?"

Toro decided to try a new process. They attempted to act quickly each time anyone was injured using a Toro product, whatever the cause. They would immediately dispatch a team to sit down with the injured person and say, "The Toro Company is really sorry this happened. What can we do to help you?" The team was authorized to pay for medical expenses, lost work time, and some amount of trauma compensation. They informed the person that they were free to contact an attorney whether or not they accepted Toro's payments. They also brought in an engineer to ask the injured person for safety suggestions and to investigate whether anything could be done to improve the product. In cases where legal action was brought against them, Toro vigorously defended itself.

Melrose's purpose was to extend Toro's excellent customer service, even in the conflict that was implicit in a potential lawsuit. Contrary to some fears about legal exposure, the new policy turned out to drastically reduce rather than increase the company's legal costs. More often than not, injured people got the help they wanted and didn't feel the need to file a lawsuit. Pleased with the team's efforts, Melrose concluded, "The best part of this is we've been able to retain these customers for life."

Food for Thought

Toro's innovative plan demonstrates that we can serve others even in the midst of conflict in our workplaces. Paul was speaking from real-world experience when he said, "Let your gentleness be shown to everyone" (Phil. 4:5). Gentleness, humbleness, peace and serving others are not signs of weakness, but signs of God's strength at work in us. Where have you seen gentleness succeed at work? Where have you seen it fail?

_____
_____
_____
_____
_____

Few of us have the ability to influence our organization's major policies and procedures the way Ken Melrose did. But all of us can find concrete ways to serve others even when we're in conflict with them. Think of a conflict at work. What resources can you access to serve the people who are in conflict?

_____
_____
_____
_____
_____
_____
_____
_____

Prayer

Jesus,

Thank you for leaders who act boldly as believers. Strengthen me with wisdom to do the same.

Amen.

Chapter 8
Truth, Love, Trust, and Effectiveness

Lesson #1: Truth and Love Build Trust

A. W. Tozer wrote in his daily devotional, "Our Lord Jesus Christ said 'I am the truth,' and in so saying he joined truth to deity in inseparable union. Thus to love God is to love the truth!" The belief that the concepts "truth" and "love" naturally combine to form a single idea finds voice in each of the three letters written by the apostle John (1 John 3:18; 2 John 1, 3; 3 John 3). According to John, love plus truth equals an environment in which grace, mercy, and peace will be with us.

Sadly, we often act as though grace, mercy, and peace depend on love *minus* truth—especially in the workplace. We may hide or shade uncomfortable truths in our communications with others in the misguided belief that telling the truth would not be loving. Or we may fear that telling the truth will lead to conflict and ill will, rather than grace or peace. Thinking we are merciful, we fail to tell the truth.

Jack Welch, a former CEO of General Electric (USA), was a controversial figure due in part to his practice of giving truthful, candid performance reviews. He let employees know on a monthly basis how well they were meeting expectations. Once a year he told them whether they were top performers, middle performers who needed to improve in specific areas, or bottom performers who were in danger of losing their jobs. Some may regard this policy as harsh, but Welch regarded it as loving:

> I've come to learn that the worst kind of manager is the one who practices false kindness. I tell people, You think you're a nice manager, that you're a kind manager? Well, guess what? You won't be there someday. You'll be promoted. Or you'll retire. And a new manager will come in and look at the employee and say, "Hey, you're not that good." And all of a sudden, this employee is now fifty-three or fifty-five, with many fewer options in life. And now you're gonna tell him, "Go home"? How is that kind? You're the cruelest kind of manager.
> ("What I've Learned," *Esquire*, December 31, 2006)

For the Christian leader, love must always begin with the truth because it is God's way and because it builds an environment of trust that promotes a healthy, productive workplace.

Food for Thought

Life in a fallen world sometimes puts the truth and love into opposition, as when Corrie Ten Boom lied to the Nazis about hiding Jews in her house; or when truth causes harm, as in telling a child a truth they are not prepared to understand. Are you facing a truth/love conflict? How do you resolve those conflicts?

_____

_____

_____

_____

_____

_____

Ephesians 4:15 calls us to speak the truth in love. What are we to do about relationships with deceitful people? We may be able to do more for the cause of truth and love by remaining engaged and telling the truth than by leaving the scene. Think of a deceitful co-worker and pray for an opportunity to be truthful with them in a way that builds them up rather than corrects them.

Prayer

Holy Spirit,

I ask that you clearly show me the true intentions of my heart that I may speak the truth in love for the highest good of others and the effectiveness of my organization.

Amen.

Lesson #2: Trust and Transparency Build Effectiveness

When there is trust, there can be transparency—the open exchange of truth. This open exchange is critical to the effective running of any enterprise of more than one person. As the saying goes, "Information is power" and that saying is especially true in the workplace.

When Ford CEO Alan Mulally was asked about how he dealt with bad news, he said:

> There is no bad news. It is just the way it is. There is a status, and you must know what the status is. So when we are going through [a review] every red and yellow [self-reported problem] is celebrated. What's not acceptable is to cover up the real status, because that just doesn't work for anybody. You can't be holding information, not saying that you have a problem, believing you can manage it in secret.
>
> You don't have days, you don't have hours, you need to know what the problem is right away in this fast-paced world. And this is particularly true in the automotive industry, where a production line of vehicles can pile up very quickly!
>
> You must make it safe to talk the truth. It is not about acting all warm and fuzzy, but you have to know everything to make good decisions, and to get there you have got to make it safe when something goes wrong. If you yell at somebody when they put a yellow up, it is going to be green next week. They are human beings. (ethix.org, July 15, 2010)

Paul might have concealed Onesimus' whereabouts, but instead he laid all his cards on the table in front of Philemon: "I prefer to do nothing without your consent" (Philem. 14). How do you create a transparent environment in your workplace? It starts at the top. It means creating a set of values that are not only talked about but lived, starting with leaders who value truth, earn trust, and reward transparency in the workplace. Paul, as a leader of the early Christians, modeled transparency so that Philemon might practice it too.

Maintaining transparency when we know our own weaknesses requires humility and the willingness to offer and accept a genuine apology. The leader who remembers that we all "have this treasure in clay jars, so that it may be made clear that this extraordinary power belongs to God and does not come from us" (2 Cor. 4:7), will encourage others to participate fully and safely in truthful and transparent work.

Food for Thought

Transparency is more than the absence of lies or even simply being honest. It is openness, done with honesty, for the sake of relationship rather than for personal gain. Transparency is honesty in action—a powerful basis for building trust and relationships. Do people in your workplace share information? What can you do to promote transparency in your workplace?

On a daily basis, we face temptation to hide the truth in ways that are not direct lies. These include obscuring motivations in order to falsely gain trust from a customer or a rival, making decisions in secret as a way of avoiding accountability or hiding factors others would object to, or pretending to support co-workers in their presence but speaking derisively behind their backs. Ask yourself this question: If your co-workers can't trust you, can God?

Prayer

Father,

It would be much easier for me to be transparent with people if I were always right. Teach me to use your strength in my weakness to help build a vital workplace of productive transparency and trust.

Amen.

Lesson #3: Godly Leadership Is Effective Leadership

Godly leadership serves God by serving people. It accomplishes organizational goals by equipping and encouraging people to do their best voluntarily and from the heart. Modeled by Paul, who himself followed Jesus' example, servant leaders put the good of others before their own interests without compromising the responsibilities they have to deliver results.

Unafraid to exercise authority when required, the godly leader often chooses to lead relationally, rather than showing off his or her rank or power. Godly leaders invest in relationships at work by acting with integrity, and telling the truth in love. This develops the trust that is foundational to a healthy, transparent, productive workplace. This approach to leadership works because it is Jesus' approach with us.

Henry Kaestner, Chairman of the investment firm Sovereign Capital, has worn many hats including entrepreneur, philanthropist, and CEO of a successful communications technology company. When CEO of that company, he intentionally established a corporate culture that promoted four priorities: God first, family second, work third, and physical exercise fourth. He was interviewed by the Center for Faith and Work for an article titled "Faith and Profit Are Not Mutually Exclusive." Asked what he sees as the biggest hurdles for leaders who want to run a company that glorifies God, he answered:

> I think the greatest hurdle is not focusing enough on their own discipleship. Running a Christ-led company comes from a transformed heart and a realization that we indeed have found a treasure in a field. We've found the pearl. We've won the jackpot. We've been given the gift of life both now and in eternity. And that changes everything about why we work and whose glory we work for. That realization fuels us with an energy and desire to work for something greater than ourselves, greater than the bottom line, greater than shareholder value, and when we do that, great things can happen.

Food for Thought

In an interview with Small Business School, Joseph Semprevivo, founder of Joseph's Lite Cookies, describes his workplace this way:

> We're team-based, and in order to have a team, you have to have honesty, integrity and promise-keeping. People need to know that [they depend on] the person to their right and to their left . . . and our team members in the front office depend on the team members in the production facility. And I would not have a job if it wasn't for my team members in production. . . . So it's a true partnership.

In what ways is managing an individual's performance different from managing a group? Does servant leadership look different in each context?

_____

_____

_____

_____

_____

_____

What have you learned from Paul and the other godly leaders in this Bible study? What new practices do you intend to take to your workplace?

_____

_____

_____

_____

Prayer

Jesus,

In Luke 11:33, you said that "no one lights a lamp and puts it in a place where it will be hidden, or under a bowl. Instead they put it on its stand, so that those who come in may see the light." I ask for your love and strength and truth to be that light as I bear your image into my workplace.

Amen.

Wisdom for Using This Study in the Workplace

Community within the workplace is a good thing and a Christian community within the workplace is even better. Sensitivity is needed, however, when we get together in the workplace (even a Christian workplace) to enjoy fellowship time together, learn what the Bible has to say about our work, and encourage one another in Jesus' name. When you meet at your place of employment, here are some guidelines to keep in mind:

- *Be sensitive to your surroundings.* Know your company policy about having such a group on company property. Make sure not to give the impression that this is a secret or exclusive group.

- *Be sensitive to time constraints.* Don't go over your allotted time. Don't be late to work! Make sure you are a good witness to the others (especially non-Christians) in your workplace by being fully committed to your work during working hours and doing all your work with excellence.

- *Be sensitive to the shy or silent members of your group.* Encourage everyone in the group and give them a chance to talk.

- *Be sensitive to the others by being prepared.* Read the Bible study material and Scripture passages and think about your answers to the questions ahead of time.

These Bible studies are based on the *Theology of Work Bible Commentary*. Besides reading the commentary, please visit the Theology of Work website (www.theologyofwork.org) for videos, interviews, and other material on the Bible and your work.

Leader's Guide

Living Word. It is always exciting to start a new group and study. The possibilities of growth and relationship are limitless when we engage with one another and with God's word. Always remember that God's word is "alive and active, sharper than any double-edged sword" (Heb. 4:12) and when you study his word, it should change you.

A Way Has Been Made. Please know you and each person joining your study have been prayed for by people you will probably never meet who share your faith. And remember that "the Lord himself goes before you and will be with you; he will never leave you nor forsake you. Do not be afraid; do not be discouraged" (Deut. 31:8). As a leader, you need to know that truth. Remind yourself of it throughout this study.

Pray. It is always a good idea to pray for your study and those involved weeks before you even begin. It is recommended to pray for yourself as leader, your group members, and the time you are about to spend together. It's no small thing you are about to start and the more you prepare in the Spirit, the better. Apart from Jesus, we can do nothing (John 14:5). Remain in him and "you will bear much fruit" (John 15:5). It's also a good idea to have trusted friends pray and intercede for you and your group as you work through the study.

Spiritual Battle. Like it or not, the Bible teaches that we are in the middle of a spiritual battle. The enemy would like nothing more than for this study to be ineffective. It would be part of his scheme to have group members not show up or engage in any discussion. His victory would be that your group just passes time together going through the motions of a yet another Bible study. You, as a leader, are a threat to the enemy, as it is your desire to lead people down the path of righteousness (as taught in Proverbs). Read Ephesians 6:10–20 and put your armor on.

Scripture. Prepare before your study by reading the selected Scripture verses ahead of time.

Chapters. Each chapter contains approximately three lessons. As you work through the lessons, keep in mind the particular chapter theme in connection with the lessons. These lessons are designed so that you can go through them in thirty minutes each.

Lessons. Each lesson has teaching points with their own discussion questions. This format should keep the participants engaged with the text and one another.

Food for Thought. The questions at the end of the teaching points are there to create discussion and deepen the connection between each person and the content being addressed. You know the people in your group and should feel free to come up with your own questions or adapt the ones provided to best meet the needs of your group. Again, this would require some preparation beforehand.

Opening and Closing Prayers. Sometimes prayer prompts are given before and usually after each lesson. These are just suggestions. You know your group and the needs present, so please feel free to pray accordingly.

Bible Commentary. The Theology of Work series contains a variety of books to help you apply the Scriptures and Christian faith to your work. This Bible study is based on the *Theology of Work Bible Commentary*, examining what the Bible says about work. This commentary is intended to assist those with theological training or interest to conduct in-depth research into passages or books of Scripture.

Video Clips. The Theology of Work website (www.theologyofwork.org) provides good video footage of people from the marketplace highlighting the teaching from all the books of the Bible. It would be great to incorporate some of these videos into your teaching time.

Enjoy your study! Remember that God's word does not return void—ever. It produces fruit and succeeds in whatever way God has intended it to succeed.

> "So shall my word be that goes out from my mouth;
>   it shall not return to me empty,
> but it shall accomplish that which I purpose,
>   and succeed in the thing for which I sent it." (Isa. 55:11)

"This commentary was written exactly for those of us who aim to integrate our faith and work on a daily basis and is an excellent reminder that God hasn't called the world to go to the church, but has called the Church to go to the world."

BONNIE WURZBACHER
FORMER SENIOR VICE PRESIDENT, THE COCA-COLA COMPANY